Slow Cooker 100% VEGAN!

Irresistibly Good & Super Easy Slow Cooker Recipes to Save Your Time & Get Healthy

By <u>Karen Greenvang</u> (aka Karen Vegan)

Copyright ©Karen Greenvang 2016

All rights reserved. No part of this publication may be reproduced, stored in a retrieval system, or transmitted, in any form or by any means, electronic, mechanical, photocopying, recording or otherwise, without the prior written permission of the author and the publishers.

The scanning, uploading, and distribution of this book via the Internet, or via any other means, without the permission of the author is illegal and punishable by law. Please purchase only authorized electronic editions, and do not participate in or encourage electronic piracy of copyrighted materials.

All information in this book has been carefully researched and checked for factual accuracy. However, the author and publishers make no warranty, expressed or implied, that the information contained herein is appropriate for every individual, situation or purpose, and assume no responsibility for errors or omission. The reader assumes the risk and full responsibility for all actions, and the author will not be held liable for any loss or damage, whether consequential, incidental, and special or otherwise, that may result from the information presented in this publication.

All cooking is an experiment in a sense, and many people come to the same or similar recipe over time. All recipes in this book have been derived from author's personal experience. Should any bear a close resemblance to those used elsewhere, that is purely coincidental.

The book is not intended to provide medical advice or to take the place of medical advice and treatment from your personal physician. Readers are advised to consult their own doctors or other qualified health professionals regarding the treatment of medical conditions. The author shall not be held liable or responsible for any misunderstanding or misuse of the information contained in this book. The information is not intended to diagnose, treat or cure any disease.

It is important to remember that the author of this book is not a doctor/ medical professional. Only opinions based upon her own personal experiences or research are cited. THE AUTHOR DOES NOT OFFER MEDICAL ADVICE or prescribe any treatments. For any health or medical issues – you should be talking to your doctor first.

Table of Contents

Introduction...6

Free Complimentary eBook from Karen...8

Breakfasts...9

Lunches...30

Soups...47

Dinners...57

Conclusion...82

More Books by Karen...85

Vegan Slow Cooker Recipes

Introduction

A slow cooker is a great kitchen investment because it provides you with the opportunity to create delicious and nutritious home cooked meals without spending hours in the kitchen. The safety and low energy consumption of a slow cooker means that you can prepare the ingredients of a dish the night before and place everything in your slow cooker first thing in the morning before leaving for work and your meal will be ready when you walk in the door at the end of the day. Of course the slow cooker can also be left to create culinary magic overnight, allowing you to wake up in the morning to a delicious hearty breakfast.

By slow cooking a meal you are retaining all the flavor, moisture and nutrients of the ingredients. As you will see with the recipes in this book, the possibilities and choices of meals that can be created using a slow cooker are endless.

There are four sections to this recipe book that will make you never want to pack your slow cooker away. We start with healthy nutritious breakfasts that will kick start your day and save you time out of your morning rush, we then go on to tasty lunches that will pick you up in the middle of the day, wholesome comforting soups will get you through the late afternoon and keep you going on until dinner where we will have some hearty, options to satisfy any type of hunger all night.

All these recipes are one hundred percent vegan and focus on using ingredients that are of the highest nutritional value. They are also easy to prepare, giving you all the inspiration you need to consistently make healthier meal choices with little effort while staying true to your very important lifestyle choice of the vegan way.

Free Complimentary eBook

Before we dive into the recipes, I would like to offer you a free, complimentary recipe eBook with delicious vegan superfood smoothies.

Download it now, before you forget:

www.bitly.com/karenfreegift

If you have any problems with your download, email me at: karenveganbooks@gmail.com

Breakfasts

We all know that breakfast is the most important meal of the day, but some days things don't always go according to plan. We sleep through our alarm or spill toothpaste on our shirts, any number of unexpected things can happen during our morning rush that will result in running late and not having time for breakfast. This is where your slow cooker will really come to good use, by preparing your breakfast the night before and leaving the slow cooker to work its magic overnight, you will never have to worry about finding time to put breakfast together in the morning. The recipes in this section include high quality slow releasing carbohydrates, healthy fats and proteins that will help you kick start your day and you metabolism the healthy way.

Coconut Quinoa with Raspberries and Almonds

Quinoa is an incredibly versatile grain that is high in amino acids, essential minerals and is considered a complete protein. Quinoa is also a slow-releasing high fibre carbohydrate, making it an excellent grain option for breakfast. Raspberries are high in antioxidants and vitamin C, they are also known for their cancer-fighting and anti-inflammatory properties. The coconut milk and almonds provide essential healthy fats and minerals.

Serves 4

Ingredients:

- 1 Cup (250ml) Raw quinoa
- 2 Cups (500ml) Coconut Milk
- 1 Cup (250ml) Fresh Raspberries
- 4 Tablespoons (60ml) Raw Almonds, roughly chopped
- 1 teaspoon (5ml) Ground cinnamon
- ½ teaspoon (2.5ml) Ground ginger
- 1 Cup (250ml) Coconut Cream, for serving

Instructions:

1. Place the raw quinoa in the dish of your slow cooker.
2. Add the ground cinnamon, ground ginger, raw almonds and fresh raspberries. Stir all together.
3. Add the coconut milk and stir well.
4. Place the lid on the slow cooker and set to low heat, leave to cook over night (approximately 8 hours)

To Serve:

1. In four separate serving bowls place ½ cup (125ml) of the cooked quinoa mix

2. Pour ¼ cup (60ml) of the coconut cream over each bowl and serve. If you have time, you can whip the coconut cream before placing it over the quinoa and sprinkling a little extra ground cinnamon over the top.

Banana Peanut Butter Oatmeal with Raw Seeds

Oats are another great choice of grain for breakfast, especially in their whole form. Oats are high in slow-releasing carbohydrates and are known for their ability to help reduce cholesterol levels. Bananas are a great source of potassium and essential minerals, and the raw seeds add a dose of healthy omega 3 fats.

Serves 4

Ingredients:

- 1 Cup (250ml) Raw oats
- 2 Cups (500ml) Oat milk
- 2 medium sized bananas, finely sliced
- 4 Tablespoons (60ml) Raw seed mix
- 1 teaspoon (5ml) Ground cinnamon
- 4 Tablespoons (60ml) Organic, natural peanut butter
- 1 Cup (250ml) Additional oat milk, for serving

Instructions:

1. Place the raw oats, ground cinnamon and raw seeds in the dish of your slow cooker.
2. Add the sliced banana and oat milk, stir all together.
3. Stir in the peanut butter.
4. Place the lid on the slow cooker and turn to a low heat.
5. Cook overnight (approximately 8 hours)

To Serve:

1. In four separate serving bowls, place ½ cup (125ml) of the cooked oats mix into each bowl.
2. Warm the additional oat milk either in the microwave or on the stove top in a saucepan.
3. Add ¼ cup (60ml) of the warm oat milk to each bowl of oats and stir well before serving.
4. Note that heating the additional oat milk is optional.

Chocolaty Oat Bran with Hazel Nuts and Strawberries

Oat bran has a higher soluble fibre content than regular oatmeal and therefore provides another very healthy grain choice for breakfast. As with oat meal, oat bran is also known for its ability to lower cholesterol, and its slow releasing carbohydrate content will keep you full and satisfied all morning. Hazel nuts provide protein, healthy fats and minerals to this dish, while the strawberries and raw cocoa add essential amino acids and anti-oxidants.

Serves 4

Ingredients:

- 1 Cup (250ml) Raw oat bran
- 2 Cups (500ml) Oat milk
- 1 Cup (250ml) Fresh strawberries, quartered
- 4 Tablespoons (60ml) Raw Hazel nuts, finely chopped
- 1 Tablespoon (15ml) Raw cocoa powder
- 1 teaspoon (5ml) Ground cinnamon

- 1 Cup (250ml) Additional oat milk, for serving

Instructions:

1. Place the raw oat bran, ground cinnamon, raw cocoa powder and hazel nuts in the dish of your slow cooker.

2. Stir in the quartered strawberries.

3. Add the oat milk and stir well.

4. Place the lid on your slow cooker and set to a low heat.

5. Cook overnight, approximately 8 hours.

To Serve:

1. In four separate serving bowls, place ½ cup (125ml) of the oat bran mix.

2. Heat the additional oat milk in the microwave or on the stove top in a saucepan.

3. Add ¼ cup (60ml) of the warm oat milk to each bowl and stir well before serving.

4. Heating of the additional oat milk is optional.

Apple Pie Oatmeal with Raisins, Almonds and Coconut Cream

Apples are high in vitamin C, minerals and fibre, making them an excellent fruit choice for breakfast since they help to maintain satiety and energy levels. Raisins are a great source of iron and the cinnamon not only adds a comforting flavor, but is also known for its blood-glucose regulating properties. Waking up to the smell of this breakfast on a winter's morning will be sure to start your day with a smile.

Serves 4

Ingredients:

- 1 Cup (250ml) Raw Oats

- 2 Cups (500ml) Oat milk

- 1 Cup (250ml) Grated fresh apple, it is recommended that you don't peel the apple before grating it as this will add to the fibre content of the meal, as well as prevent the loss of essential nutrients that are found just underneath the skin of the fruit.

- ½ Cup (125ml) Raisins

- 1 teaspoon (5ml) Ground Cinnamon

- ½ teaspoon (2.5ml) Baking spice mix

- ¼ teaspoon (1.25ml) Ground cloves

- 1 teaspoon (5ml) Vanilla essence

- 1 Cup (250ml) Coconut Cream for serving

- 4 Tablespoons (60ml) Raw almonds, finely chopped, for serving

Instructions:

1. Place the raw oats, baking spice mix, cinnamon, ground cloves and raisins in the dish of your slow cooker

2. Add the grated apple and stir all together

3. In a jug, mix the oat milk with the vanilla essence and add it to the oats mixture.

4. Stir well.

5. Place the lid on the slow cooker and set to a low heat

6. Cook over night, approximately 8 hours

To Serve:

1. Using four separate serving bowls, place ½ cup (125ml) of the cooked oat mixture in each bowl

2. Whip the coconut cream to a fluffy consistency

3. Add ¼ cup (60ml) coconut cream to each bowl of oats

4. Sprinkle 1 tablespoon (15ml) of the chopped almonds over each bowl and serve.

Coconuty Brown Rice Breakfast Pudding with Mango, Cashew Nuts and Dried Pineapple

The high fibre and B vitamin content of brown rice makes it a very versatile grain, so there is no reason why it can't form the basis of a wholesome and nutritious breakfast. Mangoes are high in vitamin C and are known to contain pre-biotics, so they are a great aid to the digestive system. The dried pineapple provides a zing to the overall flavor as well as some extra vitamins and minerals. The coconut and cashew nuts provide healthy fats that will round off this breakfast as a great slow-releasing, energizing meal.

Serves 4

Ingredients:

- 1 Cup (250ml) Raw brown rice
- 2 Cups (500ml) Coconut milk
- 1 Cup (250ml) Diced fresh mango
- 4 Tablespoon (60ml) Desiccated coconut
- 4 Tablespoons (60ml) Dried pineapple, finely chopped

- 1 teaspoon (5ml) Ground ginger

- 1 teaspoon (5ml) Vanilla essence

- 4 Tablespoons (60ml) Raw cashew nuts, roughly chopped, for serving

- 1 Cup (250mL) Coconut cream, for serving

Instructions:

1. Place the raw brown rice, ground ginger, desiccated coconut and dried pineapple into the dish of your slow cooker
2. Add the fresh mango and stir together
3. In a jug, mix the coconut milk with the vanilla essence
4. Add the coconut milk to the rice mixture and stir well
5. Place the lid on your slow cooker and cook overnight, approximately 8 hours

To Serve:

1. In four separate serving bowls, place ½ cup (250ml) of the cooked mango rice
2. Whip the coconut cream

3. Place ¼ cup (60ml) coconut cream on top of each bowl of mango rice

4. Sprinkle 1 tablespoon (15ml) of the chopped cashew nuts over each bowl and serve

Cornmeal Porridge with Dates and Seeds

Cornmeal is an excellent source of fibre and essential minerals; it also contains a small amount of healthy fats. Dates are known for their high vitamin C and iron content and the raw sees add some extra heart-healthy fats to this dish. This is a great breakfast option on a day that will involve large amounts of physical activity.

Serves 4

Ingredients:

- 1 Cup (250ml) Raw cornmeal
- 2 Cups (500ml) Almond milk
- ½ Cup (125ml) Chopped dates
- ½ Cup (125ml) Raw seed mix
- 1 teaspoon (5ml) Ground cinnamon
- 1 Cup (250ml) Additional almond milk for serving
- 4 Tablespoons (60ml) Tahini, for serving

Instructions:

1. Place the raw cornmeal, chopped dates, seed mix and cinnamon into the dish of your slow cooker, stir all together
2. Add the almond milk and stir well
3. Place the lid on your slow cooker and cook on a low heat overnight, approximately 8 hours.

To Serve:

1. Using four separate serving bowls, place ½ cup (125ml) of the cooked cornmeal porridge into each bowl
2. Heat the additional almond milk in either the microwave or a saucepan on the stovetop
3. Pour 1 Tablespoon (15ml) of the Tahini over each bowl of the cornmeal porridge
4. Pour ¼ cup (60ml) of the warm almond milk over each bowl of the cornmeal porridge and stir well before serving.
5. Heating of the additional almond milk is optional

Millet with Pear and Brazil Nuts

Millet is another versatile grain that can be enjoyed at breakfast time as well; it is known for its high magnesium content and its ability to aid in muscle tissue recovery and repair, it is also high in B vitamins. Pears are known for their high fibre content and are rich in essential vitamins and minerals. Brazil nuts not only contain heart healthy fats, but are also high in selenium and are known for their ability to help lower cholesterol.

Serves 4

Ingredients:

- 1 Cup (250ml) Raw millet
- 2 Cups (500ml) Oat milk
- 1 Cup (250ml) Diced fresh pear
- 4 Tablespoons (60ml) Raw Brazil nuts, finely chopped
- 1 Teaspoon (5ml) Ground cinnamon
- 1 Teaspoon (5ml) Vanilla essence
- 1 Cup (250ml) Additional oat milk, for serving

Instructions:

1. Place the raw millet, diced pear, brazil nuts and ground cinnamon into the dish of your slow cooker and stir together

2. In a jug, mix the oat milk with the vanilla essence

3. Add the oat milk and vanilla mixture to the millet mix and stir well

4. Place the lid on to the slow cooker

5. Cook overnight on a low heat, approximately 8 hours.

To Serve:

1. In four separate bowls, place ½ cup (125ml) of the cooked millet in each bowl

2. Heat the additional oat milk in either the microwave or a saucepan on the stove top

3. Add ¼ cup (60ml) of the warm oat milk to each bowl of millet and stir well before serving

4. Heating of the additional oat milk is optional.

"Carrot Cake" Oatmeal with Pecan Nuts and Coconut Cream

Carrots are high in vitamin A and are a great source of healthy carbohydrates, anti-oxidants and essential minerals. Pecan nuts are also high in essential minerals and are known to help lower cholesterol. This is another comforting, filling breakfast option.

Serves 4

Ingredients:

- 1 Cup (250ml) Raw Oats
- 2 Cups (500ml) Oat milk
- 1 Cup (250ml) Grated fresh carrot
- 4 Tablespoons (60ml) Raw pecan nuts, finely chopped
- ½ Cup (125ml) Golden Sultanas
- 1 teaspoon (5ml) Ground Cinnamon
- 1 teaspoon (5ml) Baking spice mix
- ½ teaspoon (2.5ml) Ground ginger

- 1 teaspoon (5ml) Vanilla essence

- 1 Cup (250ml) Coconut cream, for serving

- 4 Tablespoons (60ml) Tahini, for serving

Instructions:

1. Place the raw oats, ground cinnamon, baking spice mix, ground ginger, pecan nuts, sultanas and grated carrot into the dish of your slow cooker, stir all together.

2. In a jug, mix the oat milk with the vanilla essence

3. Add the oat milk and vanilla mix to the oats mixture and stir well.

4. Place the lid on the slow cooker

5. Cook at a low heat overnight, approximately 8 hours

To Serve:

1. In four separate serving bowls, place ½ cup (125ml) of the carrot cake oats into each bowl

2. Whip the coconut cream

3. Top each bowl of carrot cake oats with ¼ cup (60ml) whipped coconut cream

4. Drizzle 1 tablespoon (15ml) of Tahini over each bowl and serve

Lunches

In our fast-paced modern day lives we often find ourselves skipping lunch, but this is a meal that is just as important as either of the other two main meals of the day. Lunch time is when we get to take a break and re-charge our batteries in order to keep going for the rest of the day. A wholesome, nutritious and energy-sustaining meal at this time of the day is the best way to do this. The recipes in this section will give you a great midday pick-up since they all focus on providing a nutritionally balanced and filling meal that can be enjoyed hot or cold.

Quinoa with Butternut, Onion and Chickpeas

Butternut is a very versatile vegetable that is high in vitamin A and healthy carbohydrates. By cooking butternut in a slow cooker you are releasing its natural sweetness, making this dish one of those that is truly delicious either hot or cold.

Serves 4

Ingredients:

- 1 Cup (250ml) Raw Quinoa
- 4 Cups (1litre) Diced raw butternut
- 1 Can chickpeas, drained and well rinsed
- 1 teaspoon (5ml) Fresh garlic, finely chopped
- 2 medium sized onions, halved and sliced
- 1 teaspoon (5ml) Ground organic sea salt
- 1 teaspoon (5ml) Ground black pepper
- 1 teaspoon (5ml) fresh or dried rosemary
- 2 Cups (500ml) hot water

- 4 Tablespoons (60ml) Raw pumpkin seeds, for serving

Instructions:

1. Place the raw quinoa at the bottom of the dish of the slow cooker

2. In a separate bowl, mix the onions, garlic, salt, pepper, rosemary, raw butternut and chickpeas together

3. Add the butternut mix to the dish of the slow cooker

4. Add the hot water

5. Place the lid on the slow cooker

6. Cook for on a low heat for 8 hours

To serve:

1. In four separate serving bowls, place 1 cup (250ml) of the butternut quinoa dish in each bowl.

2. Sprinkle 1 tablespoon (15ml) of the raw pumpkin seeds over each bowl and serve

Egg Plant Melanzane with Black Olives and Lentils

This dish is a vegan option for the classic north Italian dish that is made up of layers of egg plant and tomatoes. By making this dish in the slow cooker you are allowing all the natural flavors, including the sweetness of the tomatoes to permeate into the egg plant and lentils. This really is a wholesome dish that can also be enjoyed hot or cold.

Serves 4

Ingredients:

- 3 large Egg plants, sliced
- 4 Cups (1litre) Fresh tomatoes, finely chopped
- 1 Can lentils, drained and well rinsed
- 1 teaspoon (5ml) Fresh garlic, finely chopped
- ½ Cup (125ml) Black olives, pitted
- 1 teaspoon (5ml) Dried Italian herb mix
- 1 teaspoon (5ml) Ground organic sea salt
- 1 teaspoon (5ml) Ground black pepper

- 1 Tablespoon (15ml) Extra virgin olive oil
- ¼ (60ml) Fresh basil leaves, finely chopped

Instructions:

1. In a bowl, mix the chopped tomatoes, garlic, dried herb mix, salt, pepper, black olives and lentils.
2. Line the base of the dish of your slow cooker with a layer of the egg plant slices
3. Cover the egg plant slices with 1 Cup (250ml) of the tomato mixture
4. Add another layer of egg plant slices
5. Add another 1cup (250ml) of the tomato mixture
6. Continue layering as such until you have used all the ingredients, but you must make sure that your top layer is one of egg plant slices
7. Drizzle the olive oil over the top and cover with the lid of the slow cooker
8. Cook on a low heat for 8 hours

To Serve:

1. Using four separate serving bowls, place a generous amount of the melanzane in each bowl

2. Sprinkle 1 tablespoon (15ml) of the fresh basil over each bowl and serve

3. It is optional to drizzle a little additional extra virgin olive oil over each bowl before serving

Mixed Vegetables with Brown Rice and Red Kidney Beans

This is a very colorful dish that is perfect for that midday pick-me-up. The variety of vegetables provides good mix of essential vitamins and minerals. Together with the brown rice and red kidney beans you have a wholesome, protein rich lunchtime meal. By cooking all these vegetables in the slow cooker you are allowing them to create their own natural stock, and flavor.

Serves 4 (but will probably have leftovers)

Ingredients:

- 1 Cup (250ml) Raw carrot, sliced
- 1 Cup (250ml) Raw cauliflower florets
- 1 Cup (250ml) Raw zucchini, sliced
- 1 Cup (250ml) Raw broccoli florets
- 1 Cup (250ml) Fresh, or frozen peas
- 1 Cup (250ml) Fresh, or frozen sweet corn kernals
- 1 Can Red kidney beans, drained and well rinsed

- 1 teaspoon (5ml) Fresh Garlic, finely chopped

- 1 teaspoon (5ml) Dried Italian herb mix

- 1 teaspoon (5ml) Ground organic sea salt

- 1 teaspoon (5ml) Ground black pepper

- 1 Cup (250ml) Raw brown rice

- 2 Cups (500ml) Hot water

- 4 Tablespoon (60ml) Raw seed mix, for serving

Instructions:

- Place the raw brown rice in the bottom of the slow cooker dish

- In a separate bowl, mix all the vegetables, red kidney beans, garlic, herbs, salt and pepper.

- Add the vegetables to the slow cooker dish

- Add the hot water

- Cover with the lid and cook on a low heat for 8 hours

To Serve:

1. Using four separate serving bowls, place 1 cup (250ml) of the cooked vegetables in each bowl.

2. Sprinkle 1 tablespoon (15ml) of the raw seed mix over each bowl and serve

Wild Rice with Tofu, Spinach, Black Olives and Red Onion

It's a well known fact that spinach is high in the essential mineral iron; it is also a very tasty and versatile leafy vegetable. Red onions are high vitamins and essential minerals, and they add a little extra color to this dish. The black olives add their unique flavor along with a dose of heart healthy fats. This dish does require a little extra pre-preparation in the form of browning the tofu and toasting the pine nuts.

Serves 4:

Ingredients:

- 4 Cups (1 liter) Fresh spinach leaves
- 4 Cups (1 liter) Firm tofu, diced
- 1 Tablespoon (15ml) Extra virgin olive oil
- ½ Cup (125ml) Black olives, pitted
- 2 Medium sized red onions, halved and sliced
- 1 teaspoon (5ml) Fresh garlic, finely chopped

- 1 teaspoon (5ml) Dried Italian herb mix

- 1 teaspoon (5ml) Ground organic sea salt

- 1 teaspoon (5ml) Ground black pepper

- 1 Cup (250ml) Raw wild rice

- 2 Cups (500ml) Hot water

- 4 Tablespoons (60ml) Raw pine nuts, for serving

Instructions:

1. First brown the tofu by heating the olive oil in a wok and frying up the tofu until it has a golden brown finish, set aside.

2. Place the raw wild rice in the bottom of the slow cooker dish

3. In a separate bowl, toss the raw spinach with the garlic, herbs, black olives, salt and pepper

4. Add tofu to the spinach mix and toss again

5. Add the tofu/spinach mix to the slow cooker dish

6. Pour over the hot water and cover with the lid

7. Cook on a low heat for 8 hours

8. While the slow cooker is going, toast the pine nuts in a dry non-stick pan until they are golden brown, set aside for garnishing the meal when serving

To Serve:

1. Using four separate serving bowls, place a desired amount of the cooked tofu and spinach in each bowl

2. Sprinkle 1 tablespoon (15ml) of the toasted pine nuts over each bowl and serve

Couscous with Tomato, Butter Beans, Sweet Peppers and Black Olives

Couscous is a good source of essential nutrients, fibre and protein and is a very versatile grain. The butter beans add extra protein and fibre and the combination of tomato and sweet peppers make this meal very high in vitamin C.

Serves 4

Ingredients:

- 1 Cup (250ml) Raw Couscous

- 4 Cups (1 litre) Raw cherry tomatoes, halved

- 4 Cups (1 litre) Mixed sweet peppers (red, yellow, orange) chopped

- 1 teaspoon (5ml) Fresh garlic, finely chopped

- ½ Cup (125ml) Black olives, pitted

- 1 teaspoon (5ml) Dried Italian herb mix

- 1 teaspoon (5ml) Ground organic sea salt

- 1 teaspoon (5ml) Ground black pepper

- 1 Tablespoon (15ml) Extra virgin olive oil
- 1 Cup (250ml) Hot water

Instructions:

1. Place the couscous on the bottom of the slow cooker dish and drizzle with the olive oil
2. In a separate bowl, mix the tomatoes, sweet peppers, butter beans, garlic, dried herbs, salt, pepper and black olives
3. Add the vegetable and butter bean mix to the slow cooker dish
4. Add the hot water
5. Cover with the lid and cook on a low heat for 8 hours

To Serve:

1. Before serving you'll need to stir the dish in order to break up the couscous into grains
2. In four separate serving bowls, place the desired amount of the meal and serve
3. It is optional to drizzle a little extra virgin olive oil over each bowl before serving

Whole Wheat Fusilli with Ratatouille, Red Kidney Beans and Black Olives

Whole wheat pasta is a much healthier and nutritious option to the regular, highly refined white pastas. Ratatouille is a very versatile dish that combines a variety of vegetables, making it very high in essential vitamins and minerals. This is another one of those dishes that can be enjoyed either hot or cold.

Serves 4

Ingredients:

- 1 Cup (250ml) Raw whole wheat fusilli
- 1 Can Red kidney beans, drained and well rinsed
- 1 Cup (250ml) Raw egg plant, diced
- 1 Cup (250ml) Raw zucchini, sliced
- 2 Cups (500ml) Raw cherry tomatoes, halved
- 1 Cup (250ml) Mixed sweet peppers (red, yellow and orange) chopped
- ½ Cup (125ml) Black olives, pitted
- 1 Large onion, finely chopped

- 1 teaspoon (5ml) Fresh garlic, finely chopped
- 1 teaspoon (5ml) Ground organic sea salt
- 1 teaspoon (5ml) Ground black pepper
- 1 teaspoon (5ml) Dried Italian herb mix
- 1 Cup (250ml) Hot water

Instructions:

1. Place the raw fusilli in the bottom of the slow cooker dish
2. In a separate bowl, mix the red kidney beans, egg plant, zucchini, tomatoes, sweet peppers, garlic, dried herbs, black olives, salt and pepper
3. Add the vegetables to the slow cooker dish
4. Add the hot water
5. Cover with the lid and cook for 8 hours on a low heat setting

To Serve:

1. Using four separate serving bowls place the desired amount of ratatouille in each bowl and serve.

2. It is optional to drizzle a little extra virgin olive oil over each bowl before serving.

Soups

Soup is one of the ultimate comfort foods and even though we tend to mainly serve them in the winter months, there is actually no reason why we can't enjoy them all year round. What makes a homemade soup such a healthy meal option is that by making it yourself you are avoiding the high sodium and preservative content of commercially made convenience soups. These recipes will show how your slow cooker will turn soup making into one the most convenient and time saving ways of cooking. Soups are also easy to freeze, providing you with a healthy meal option that is quick and easy to defrost any time you need it.

Hearty Minestrone Soup

You can never go wrong with a good old minestrone soup. This recipe is packed with flavor and variety that will guarantee you a well-rounded healthy, balanced meal. What makes this recipe even more appealing is that every time you heat it up, the flavor will improve.

Serves 4-8

Ingredients:

- 1 Cup (250ml) Raw carrot, diced
- 1 Cup (250ml) Raw celery, sliced
- 1 Cup (250ml) Raw turnip, diced
- 1 Cup (250ml) Raw leeks, finely chopped
- 2 Cups (500ml) Raw tomatoes, finely chopped
- 1 Cup (250ml) Raw mushrooms (these can be any variety of your choosing)
- 1 Can Red kidney beans, drained and well rinsed
- ½ Cup (125ml) Celery leaves, finely chopped

- 1 Tablespoon (15ml) Fresh coriander, finely chopped
- 1 Tablespoon (15ml) Fresh garlic, finely chopped
- 1 teaspoon (5ml) Ground organic sea salt
- 1 teaspoon (5ml) Ground black pepper
- 1 teaspoon (5ml) Dried herb mix
- 4 Cups (1litre) Hot water

Instructions:

1. Place all the vegetables and the red kidney beans in the slow cooker dish
2. Add the garlic, dried herbs, salt, pepper, celery and coriander leaves
3. Cover the vegetables with the hot water
4. Place the lid on the slow cooker and cook on a low heat setting for 8-12 hours. The longer you allow it to simmer, the better the flavor will be

To Serve:

1. Place 1 cup (250ml) of minestrone soup in each of your serving bowls

2. Serve with a whole grain bread of your choice.

Coconuty Butternut Soup with Cashew Nuts

This is a very comforting soup to enjoy anytime on a cold winter's day. The butternut provides you with healthy carbohydrates and vitamin A, while the chick peas add the protein. The flavor of the coconut milk, combined with chili and lime will keep you going back for more. This soup will need to be put through the blender once it is finished cooking, since it is best served with a smooth consistency.

Serves 4-8

Ingredients:

- 4 Cups (1litre) Raw butternut, diced
- 1 Can chickpeas, drained and well rinsed
- 4 Cups (1litre) Coconut milk
- 1 Tablespoon (15ml) red chili, finely chopped
- 1 Tablespoon (15ml) Fresh garlic, finely chopped
- 1 Tablespoon (15ml) Fresh ginger, finely chopped
- 1 Tablespoon (15ml) Freshly squeezed lime juice

- 1 Tablespoon (15ml) Grated lime zest

- 4- 8 Tablespoons (60-120ml) Raw cashew nuts, finely chopped, for serving

- 4-8 Tablespoons (60-120ml) Coconut cream, for serving

Instructions:

1. In a bowl, mix the butternut, chickpeas, garlic, chili, lime zest and ginger together

2. Place the butternut mixture in the slow cooker dish

3. Add the coconut milk and lime juice, stir well

4. Place the lid on the slow cooker

5. Cook at a low heat setting for at least 10 hours, until the butternut is so soft that it is falling apart

6. Once the soup has cooled enough, place it in a blender or food processor and blend until smooth

7. Return the soup to the slow cooker dish and turn it onto a high heat until the soup comes back to a simmer and is hot enough to serve

To Serve;

1. Place 1 cup (125ml) of the butternut soup into each serving bowl

2. Swirl 1 tablespoon (15ml) of coconut cream over the centre of each bowl

3. Sprinkle 1 tablespoon (15ml) of the chopped cashew nuts over the coconut cream swirl of each bowl

4. Serve with a whole grain bread of your choice

Roasted Sweet Pepper and Tomato Soup with Lentils

With the main ingredients of this soup being the sweet peppers and tomatoes, it is very high in vitamin C, making it an excellent choice for winter. This soup does require a little pre-preparation in the form of roasting the peppers, but it really is so worth it as it brings out the sweetness of the peppers. This is also another soup that will be best served with a smooth consistency and so will require blending once it is cooked.

Serves 4-8

Ingredients:

- 4 Cups (1 litre) Mixed sweet peppers, chopped
- 4 Cups (1 litre) Cherry tomatoes, halved
- 1 Can lentils, drained and well rinsed
- 1 Tablespoon (15ml) Extra virgin olive oil
- 1 Tablespoon (15ml) Fresh garlic, finely chopped
- 1 Tablespoon (15ml) Fresh basil leaves, finely chopped

- 1 Teaspoon (5ml) Fresh, or dried rosemary

- 1 Teaspoon (5ml) Ground organic sea salt

- 1 Teaspoon (5ml) Ground black pepper

- 4 Cups (1litre) Hot water

- 4-8 Tablespoons (60-120ml) Black olives, pitted, for serving

Instructions:

1. Preheat the oven to 350 degrees (200 degrees Celsius)

2. Place the chopped peppers, tomatoes, garlic, basil, rosemary, salt and pepper into a roasting dish and drizzle over the olive oil

3. Roast the vegetables in the oven for 1 hour

4. When the hour is done, turn the oven off and allow the vegetables to cool in the oven

5. Once all has cooled, place the vegetables into the slow cooker dish

6. Add the lentils

7. Add the hot water

8. Cover with the lid and cook for 8-10 hours

9. Once the soup has cooled, place it into a blender or food processor and blend until smooth

10. Return the soup to the slow cooker dish and set on a high heat until the soup returns to a simmer and is hot enough to serve

To Serve:

1. Pour 1 cup (250ml) of the soup into each serving bowl

2. Top each bowl of soup with 1 tablespoon (15ml) of the black olives

3. This soup is best served with olive ciabatta bread, but can be served with any whole grain bread of your choice.

Dinners

Dinner time is a special time of the day because it generally is the only meal time that the whole family can share. The recipes in this section will give you inspiration to use your slow cooker for one of its most convenient uses; having dinner ready when you walk in the door at the end of the day. The wholesome, well balanced meal options that follow will ensure your family is well fed and sustained for long fast of sleeping.

Tofu Curry with Pineapple and Cashew Nuts

Coming home to the smell of this coconuty curry at the end of the day will be sure to have your stomach growling before you even open the front door. This recipe does require some pre-preparation in the form of browning the tofu. In this instance it's best to cook the rice separately, but if that's all you have to do when you get home, then this is still an easy and convenient dinner option.

Serves 4

Ingredients:

- 4 Cups (1litre) Firm tofu

- 1 Tablespoon (15ml) Organic coconut oil

- 1 Cup (250ml) Raw carrot, sliced

- 1 Cup (250ml) Raw green beans, julienned

- 1 Cup (250ml) Raw cauliflower florets, finely sliced

- 1 Cup (250ml) Fresh pineapple, diced

- ½ Cup (125ml) Spring onion, finely chopped

- 1 Teaspoon (5ml) Fresh garlic, finely chopped
- 1 Teaspoon (5ml) Fresh ginger, finely chopped
- 1 Teaspoon (5ml) Fresh red chili, finely chopped
- 1 Teaspoon (5ml) Fresh green chili, finely chopped
- ½ Cup (125ml) Whole raw cashew nuts
- 4 Cups (1 litre) Coconut Milk
- 4 Tablespoons (60ml) Freshly squeezed lime juice
- 1 Tablespoon (15ml) Grated lime zest
- 1 Cup (250ml) Brown Basmati Rice
- 2 Cups (500ml) Boiling water
- 1 Teaspoon (5ml) Salt
- 4 Tablespoons (60ml) Desiccated coconut, for serving

Instructions:

1. First brown the tofu by heating the coconut oil in a wok or frying pan, once the oil is hot add the tofu and fry until golden brown and slightly crispy.

2. Place the vegetables, chilies, cashew nuts, pineapple, lime zest, ginger and garlic the dish of your slow cooker

3. Add the browned tofu and stir all together

4. Add the coconut milk and lime juice, stir all together

5. Place the lid on the slow cooker and set to a low heat

6. Cook for 6-8 hours

To cook the rice:

1. Boil the kettle

2. Place the rice in a saucepan and add the salt

3. Pour the 2 cups (500ml) of boiling water over the rice, cover the saucepan with the lid and bring it to the boil

4. Once the rice is boiling, turn the heat down and let it simmer at a low heat until the rice has absorbed all the water and is light and fluffy, this will take about 45-50 minutes.

To Serve:

1. In four separate serving bowls, place ½ cup (125ml) of the cooked brown basmati rice in each bowl

2. Add 1 Cup (250ml) of the curry to each bowl

3. Sprinkle 1 tablespoon (15ml) of the desiccated coconut over each bowl and serve

Vegetable Curry with Dried Apricots and Red Kidney Beans

This curry is inspired by the traditional cooking of the Cape Malay culture of South Africa. The unique blend of spicy and sweet creates a hearty and comforting dinner. The combination of ingredients makes this a very nutritious and well balanced meal that will be a great dinner option at any time of the year. This dish can be served with either brown basmati rice or quinoa, and it is best to cook the grain of your choice separately.

Serves 4

Ingredients:

- 1 Cup (250ml) Raw sweet potato, diced
- 1 Cup (250ml) Raw butternut, diced
- 1 Cup (250ml) Raw cauliflower florets, sliced
- 1 Can Red kidney beans, drained and well rinsed
- 1 Cup (250ml) Dried apricot halves
- 1 Tablespoon (15ml) Apricot jam or preserve

- 1 large onion, finely chopped
- 1 Tablespoon (15ml) Coconut oil
- 1 Teaspoon (5ml) Fresh garlic, finely chopped
- 1 Teaspoon (5ml) Fresh ginger, finely chopped
- 1 Teaspoon (5ml) Ground cinnamon
- 1 Teaspoon (5ml) Masala curry spice mix
- ½ Teaspoon (2.5ml) Cumin Seeds
- ½ Teaspoon (2.5ml) Ground coriander
- 1 Cup (250ml) Brown basmati rice or quinoa
- 2 Cups (500ml) Boiling water
- 1 Teaspoon (5ml) Salt
- 4 Tablespoons (60ml) Desiccated coconut, for serving

Instructions:

1. Heat the coconut oil in a frying pan and add the onion, garlic, ginger, cinnamon, Masala mix, cumin seeds and ground coriander. Fry all together until the onion turns transparent

2. Turn the heat of the pan down to medium and add the apricot jam, stirring constantly until the jam has become slightly runny in consistency and has coated the onion mixture. Remove from the heat and set aside

3. Place the vegetables, red kidney beans and dried apricots into the dish of the slow cooker

4. Add the onion mixture and stir well

5. Place the lid on the slow cooker and set to a low heat

6. Cook for at least 8 hours

To cook the brown basmati rice or quinoa:

1. Boil the kettle

2. Place the brown basmati rice or quinoa in a saucepan and add the salt

3. Add 2 Cups (500ml) of boiling water to the saucepan and bring to the boil

4. Turn the heat down to low and allow the grain of choice to simmer until all the water has been absorbed and it is light and fluffy.

To Serve:

1. Using four separate serving bowls, place ½ cup (125ml) of the cooked rice or quinoa in each bowl

2. Add 1 Cup (250ml) of the curry to each bowl

3. Sprinkle 1 tablespoon (15ml) of desiccated coconut over each bowl and serve

Vegetable Pot Pie

This meal has it all, the variety of vegetables, healthy slow-releasing carbohydrates, protein and fats, which makes it the perfect dinner option the night before a very active day, or sporting event. This vegetable pie is also very delicious served cold as a left-over for lunch.

Serves 4-8

Ingredients:

- 1 Cup (250ml) Raw brown rice

- 1 Can Red kidney beans, drained and well rinsed

- 1 Large sweet potato, sliced (it is not necessary to peel the potatoes, as this adds to the rustic feel of the dish)

- 1 Cup (250ml) Raw butternut, diced

- 2 Cups (500ml) Raw button mushrooms, sliced

- 1 Cup (250ml) Raw cherry tomatoes, halved

- 1 Cup (250ml) Fresh or frozen peas

- 1 Cup (250ml) Fresh or frozen sweet corn kernels

- 1 medium onion, finely chopped
- 1 Cup (250 ml) Black olives, pitted and halved
- 1 Teaspoon (5ml) Fresh garlic, finely chopped
- 1 Teaspoon (5ml) Dried Italian herb mix
- 1 Teaspoon (5ml) Ground organic sea salt
- 1 Teaspoon (5ml) Ground black pepper

Instructions:

1. Place the raw brown rice in the base of the slow cooker dish
2. Cover the rice with the mushrooms
3. Cover the mushrooms with the tomatoes and red kidney beans
4. In a separate bowl, mix the onion, garlic, dried herb mix, salt and pepper, and spread it over the tomato layer
5. Cover the tomato layer with the peas and sweet corn kernels
6. Cover the pea and sweet corn layer with the black olives

7. Lastly layer the sliced sweet potato over the top of the dish

8. Place the lid on the slow cooker and turn on to a low heat

9. Cook for at least 10 hours

To Serve:

1. Place 1 Cup (250ml) of the vegetable pot pie in each serving bowl, making sure that each serving consists of all the layers of the pie.

2. It is optional to drizzle a little extra virgin olive oil over the top of each serving

Pumpkin Pie with Chickpeas and Couscous

This makes for a very comforting meal. Pumpkin is high in essential minerals and healthy carbohydrates, the pumpkin seeds provide a concentrated source of protein, vitamins and minerals as well. This is another of those dishes that can be enjoyed hot or cold, so any leftovers make a great lunch box meal.

Serves 4-8

Ingredients:

- 4 Cups (1litre) Raw pumpkin, finely diced
- 1 Can chickpeas, drained and well rinsed
- 1 Cup (250ml) Raw couscous
- 1 Tablespoon (15ml) Ground cinnamon
- 4 Tablespoons (40ml) Tahini, for serving
- 4 Tablespoons (40ml) Raw pumpkin seeds, for serving
- 4 Tablespoons (40ml) Raw sunflower seeds, for serving

Instructions:

1. Place the raw couscous in the base of the slow cooker dish

2. In a separate bowl, mix the pumpkin with the chickpeas and ground cinnamon

3. Add the pumpkin and chickpea mix to the slow cooker dish, making sure that all the couscous is covered with the pumpkin mix

4. Place the lid on the slow cooker and set to a low heat

5. Cook for 10 hours

To Serve

1. Using separate serving bowls, place approximately 1 cup (250ml) of the pumpkin pie in each bowl, making sure that each serving includes the couscous from the bottom of the pie.

2. Drizzle 1 tablespoon (15ml) of Tahini over each bowl

3. Sprinkle 1 tablespoon (15ml) of the raw pumpkin seeds over each bowl

4. Sprinkle 1 tablespoon (15ml) of the raw sunflower seeds over each bowl

5. Serve

Black Mushroom, Lentil and Potato Bake

Black mushrooms have a distinct flavor that makes them a delicious addition to any recipe, the black fungus is known to improve circulation and lower cholesterol. Potatoes are a great source of healthy carbohydrate, and are incredibly versatile since they take on and enhance the other flavors of this dish.

Serves 4-8

Ingredients:

- 4 large potatoes, sliced (it is not necessary to peel the potatoes, as this gives the dish a rustic feel)
- 4 Cups (1 liter) Black mushrooms, sliced
- 1 Can lentils, drained and well rinsed
- 1 Teaspoon (5ml) Fresh garlic, finely chopped
- 1 Teaspoon (5ml) Dried Italian herb mix
- 1 Teaspoon (5ml) Dried or fresh rosemary
- 1 Teaspoon (5ml) Ground Organic sea salt
- 1 Teaspoon (5ml) Ground black pepper

- 1 large onion, finely chopped
- 1 Tablespoon (15ml) Extra virgin olive oil

Instructions:

1. In a bowl, mix the sliced mushrooms, lentils, chopped onion, garlic, herbs, salt and pepper
2. Line the dish of the slow cooker with a layer of sliced potato
3. Cover the first layer of potato with 1 cup (250ml) of the mushroom mix
4. Cover the layer of mushroom mix with another layer of sliced potato
5. Cover the sliced potato with another cup (250ml) of the mushroom mix
6. Continue to layer as such until you have used all your ingredients, making sure that your top layer is one of potato.
7. Drizzle the olive oil over the top layer
8. Place the lid on the slow cooker and set to a low heat
9. Cook for 8 to 10 hours

To Serve:

1. Place 1 cup (250ml) of the mushroom potato bake into each serving bowl

2. It is optional to drizzle a little extra virgin olive oil over each bowl before serving.

Whole Wheat Spaghetti Bake with Mushrooms, Zucchini and Black Olives

Whole wheat spaghetti is a much healthier, high fiber alternative to the usual white, highly-refined variety. The slow releasing carbohydrate content of this dish will keep your whole family satisfied throughout the night. This is another versatile meal that can be enjoyed hot or cold and so any leftovers will make a great lunch box meal.

Serves 4-8

Ingredients:

- 1 Cup (250ml) Raw whole wheat spaghetti
- 1 Cup (250ml) Black mushrooms, sliced
- 1 Cup (250ml) White button mushrooms, sliced
- 1 Cup (250ml) Zucchini, sliced
- 1 Cup (250ml) Fresh cherry tomatoes, halved
- 1 Can Butter beans, drained and well rinsed
- 1 Cup (250ml) Fresh or frozen peas
- 1 Cup (250ml) Fresh or frozen sweet corn kernels

- 1 Cup (250ml) Black olives, pitted and sliced
- 1 Teaspoon (5ml) Fresh garlic, finely chopped
- 1 Large onion, finely chopped
- 1 Teaspoon (5ml) Dried Italian herb mix
- 1 Teaspoon (5ml) Fresh or dried rosemary
- 1 Teaspoon (5ml) Ground organic sea salt
- 1 Teaspoon (5ml) Ground black pepper
- 4 Tablespoons (60ml) Raw pine nuts

Instructions:

1. Place the raw whole wheat spaghetti in the base of the slow cooker dish, you might have to break it up a little to make it fit

2. In a bowl mix the mushrooms, zucchini, tomatoes, butter beans, peas, corn, black olives, onion, garlic, herbs, salt and pepper.

3. Place the vegetable mix on top of the spaghetti in the slow cooker dish

4. Cover the dish with its lid and set to a low heat

5. Cook for 8-10 hours

6. Toast the raw pine nuts in a dry non-stick pan until they have darkened in colour

To Serve:

1. Place 1 cup (250ml) of the mushroom spaghetti into each serving bowl

2. Sprinkle 1 tablespoon (15ml) of the toasted pine nuts over each bowl and serve

Curried Rice and Lentil Bake

This dish is inspired by the traditional Hindi dish of biryani. It is a warm and comforting meal that is high in slow releasing carbohydrates, healthy fats and protein. This recipe provides another meal option that can be enjoyed hot or cold, making the leftovers a great option for a lunchbox. This is a rather spicy dish, so if you're not too keen on the heat then you can leave out the chilies and only use the Masala mix

Serves 4-8

Ingredients:

- 2 Cups (500ml) Raw Basmati rice
- 1 Cup (250ml) Raw potato, diced
- 1 Can lentils, drained and well rinsed
- 1 Cup (250ml) Fresh or frozen sweet corn kernels
- 1 Cup (250ml) Raw Carrot, diced
- 1 Cup (250ml) Fresh or frozen peas
- 1 Cup (250ml) Button mushrooms, sliced
- 4 Cups (1litre) Hot water

- 1 Tablespoon (15ml) Fresh garlic, finely chopped
- 1 Tablespoon (15ml) Fresh ginger, finely chopped
- 1 Teaspoon (5ml) Fresh red chili, finely chopped
- 1 Teaspoon (5ml) Fresh green chili, finely chopped
- 1 Teaspoon (5ml) Mild Masala mix
- ½ Teaspoon (2.5ml) Cumin seeds
- 1 Teaspoon (5ml) Ground coriander
- 4 Tablespoons (60ml) Extra Virgin Coconut oil
- 4 Tablespoons (60ml) Raw Seed mix, for serving
- 4 Tablespoons (60ml) Fresh coriander, finely chopped, for serving
- 4 Tablespoons (60ml) Fruit chutney, for serving

Instructions:

1. In a bowl, mix the raw basmati rice, potato, lentils, carrots, peas, corn, mushrooms, ginger, garlic, chilies, Masala mix, cumin seeds and coriander
2. Toss in the coconut oil

3. Place all the mixed ingredients into the dish of the slow cooker

4. Add the hot water and stir all together

5. Place the lid on the slow cooker and set to a low heat

6. Cook for 10 to 12 hours, ideally the rice will have absorbed all the water and will be light and fluffy

To Serve:

1. Place 1 cup (250ml) of the rice and lentil bake into each serving bowl

2. Pour 1 tablespoon (15ml) of the fruit chutney over each serving

3. Sprinkle 1 tablespoon (25ml) of the raw seed mix over each bowl

4. Sprinkle 1 Tablespoon (15ml) of the fresh chopped coriander over each bowl and serve.

Your Free Gift

Don't forget to download your free complimentary

www.bitly.com/karenfreegift

If you have any problems with your download, email me at: karenveganbooks@gmail.com

I am here to help.

Conclusion

Thank you for reading!

I hope that with so many easy recipes you will be motivated and inspired to start your journey towards meaningful veganism, vibrant health and total wellbeing.

Remember, the beauty of incorporating nutritious vegan foods into your daily diet is that you are making simple, yet sustainable changes that will work for your wellness long-term. Not to mention your spiritual wellness and taking care of the environment and the animals. I wish I had known more about this lifestyle years ago! The transition can be a challenge, but trust me, it's worth it. You will love it! If you need more help, motivation, tips or recipes, I am always happy to help.

If you enjoyed my book, it would be greatly appreciated if you left a review so others can receive the same benefits you have. Your review can help other people take this important step to take care of their health and inspire them to start a new vegan chapter in their lives.

At the same time, <u>you can help me serve you and all my other readers</u> even more through my next vegan-friendly recipe books that I am committed to writing on a regular basis.

I'd be thrilled to hear from you. I would love to know your favorite recipe(s).

Don't be shy, post a comment on Amazon! I love reading reviews from my readers as they always inspire me to write more and better.

You see, I am just a small author and I can't afford a big publishing/PR or marketing company to promote me. I am really

passionate about my vegan health & wellness message and your short review could help me spread it and inspire more people!

Thank You

→ Questions about this book? Email me at: karenveganbooks@gmail.com

Thank You for your time,

Love & Light,

Until next time-

Karen Vegan Greenvang

More Vegan Books by Karen

Available in kindle and paperback in all Amazon stores:

www.amazon.com/author/karengreenvang

www.ingramcontent.com/pod-product-compliance
Lightning Source LLC
Chambersburg PA
CBHW071752080526
44588CB00013B/2218